THE RISE OF INDUSTRY: 1870-1900

by Amy Van Zee

Content Consultant
David Bensman
Professor of Labor Studies and Employment Relations
Rutgers University

CORE
LIBRARY

Published by ABDO Publishing Company, PO Box 398166, Minneapolis, MN 55439. Copyright © 2014 by Abdo Consulting Group, Inc. International copyrights reserved in all countries. No part of this book may be reproduced in any form without written permission from the publisher. The Core Library™ is a trademark and logo of ABDO Publishing Company.

Printed in the United States of America,
North Mankato, Minnesota
092013
012014

 THIS BOOK CONTAINS AT LEAST 10% RECYCLED MATERIALS.

Editor: Lauren Coss
Series Designer: Becky Daum

Library of Congress Control Number: 2013945669

Cataloging-in-Publication Data
Van Zee, Amy.
 The rise of industry: 1870-1900 / Amy Van Zee.
   p. cm. -- (The story of the United States)
Includes bibliographical references and index.
ISBN 978-1-62403-176-2
1. Industries--United States--History--Juvenile literature. 2. Industries--United States--Juvenile literature. 3. Industrial revolution--United States--History--Juvenile literature. 4. United States--Social life and customs--To 1900--Juvenile literature.   I. Title.
338.0973--dc23

                                                    2013945669

Cover: Steel workers in Pittsburgh, Pennsylvania

CONTENTS

CHAPTER ONE

RAILS AND BOOMING BUSINESS

The US government and private businessmen spent millions of dollars to build the first US transcontinental railroad. Thousands of workers blasted through rock to make its way. They labored in sweltering heat and bitter cold to lay its rails. Finally, on May 10, 1869, the railroad was completed. The Union Pacific Railroad from the east connected with

When finished in 1869, the transcontinental railroad would connect the eastern and western parts of the United States.

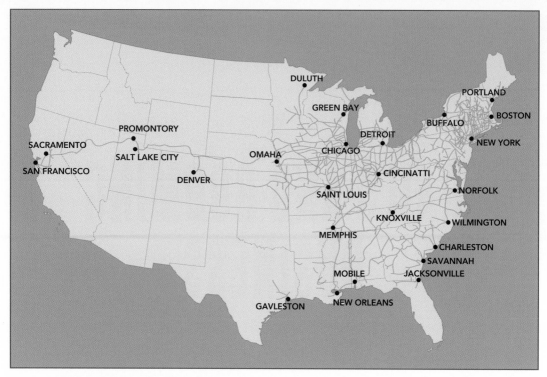

US Railroad Lines, 1870

The transcontinental railroad stretched from Omaha, Nebraska, to Sacramento, California. But railroads had already been expanding quickly in the east. How does this map help you understand how people spread across the United States in 1870? List a few ways you think the growing railroads changed US business at the time.

the Central Pacific Railroad from the west. The two railroads met in Promontory, Utah.

Time to Rebuild

Earlier in the decade, the US Civil War had nearly torn the nation apart. From 1861 to 1865, the South

The US government hoped the transcontinental railroad would encourage settlers to move to the western part of the country.

fought to become independent from the United States. The North fought to keep the nation together. Slavery was one of the main issues dividing the country. Many people in the North wanted to ban slavery. Most white Southerners supported using slave labor. The war raged for four years. In April 1865, Southern General Robert E. Lee surrendered to Northern General Ulysses S. Grant. The conflict was over. It was time to rebuild the country.

The government thought a cross-country railroad would help rebuild the nation. Railroad construction created jobs. It also brought money to the industries making the materials needed to build the railroad. The railroad connected the country. Goods made in one part of the country could be spread to other places. People could easily move from one place to another as well. The railroad would bring people to the West to settle the land.

A Lighting Revolution

For centuries, fire and candles were the main sources of light from sunset to sunrise. In the early 1800s, whale oil provided lamp fuel. But it was very costly. In the mid-1800s kerosene became available. Many social changes happened as a result. Work could now be done at night. Households could stay up working, reading, or socializing after the sun went down. Factories could stay open around the clock. People could now work longer hours.

The Titans of Oil and Steel

The rail system also helped the growth of the oil and steel industries. These were important US industries in the late 1800s. Oil was highly valued because it was used for lighting. Crude oil found in the ground

A steel worker uses a Bessemer steel converter. The Bessemer process allowed companies to make steel more easily and cheaply.

could be made into kerosene. Kerosene was burned in lamps to produce light. Trains carried kerosene to faraway customers. This made oil a national industry.

John D. Rockefeller was at the center of the US oil industry. Rockefeller spent the 1860s growing his oil business. He took any steps he needed to beat his competitors. He cut costs to grow profits.

John D. Rockefeller

Rockefeller began his career as a bookkeeper in Cleveland, Ohio, in 1855. After oil was discovered in Pennsylvania in 1859, Rockefeller found a new calling. During the US Civil War, Rockefeller made a name for himself in the oil business. He built his first oil refinery in the 1860s.

Other oil companies could not match Rockefeller's prices. Many went out of business. In 1870 Rockefeller's Standard Oil Company was founded. It was the largest oil refinery in the United States.

The demand for metal was also rising. Before the 1860s, iron was mainly used to build rails, bridges, and other industrial products. Then in the 1850s, businessman and inventor Henry Bessemer found a new way to make steel. Before then, steel took days to create. Now it could be made in minutes. Steel was stronger than iron. It also cost less. In the 1860s, steel began taking the place of iron.

In 1872 businessman Andrew Carnegie learned about Bessemer's new process for making steel. Carnegie thought he could make a great deal of

Andrew Carnegie

money by making steel in large amounts. He joined
with other businessmen. They opened a steel plant
near Pittsburgh, Pennsylvania. It was an ideal location.
Pittsburgh was near coal and iron ore mines, which are
needed to make steel. Railroads bordered the plant.
They were used to transport the coal and iron ore into
the plant. They also moved the steel out. Carnegie
was ready to become a major US steel producer.

Many banks closed during the financial depression that became known as the Panic of 1873.

Depression Hits

Carnegie and Rockefeller found great success. But much of the rest of the country was less fortunate. In 1873 major bank Jay Cooke and Company failed. This event along with others sent the nation into a financial crisis. More banks began failing. The United States went into a financial depression. Many businesses

EXPLORE ONLINE

This chapter begins with the creation of the transcontinental railroad. The Web site below discusses the work that went into building the railroad. Compare the Web site's information with the information in this chapter. What is the same? What new information did you learn from the Web site? How does the information on the Web site help you better understand the railroad?

The Transcontinental Railroad
www.mycorelibrary.com/rise-of-industry

closed. This put many Americans out of work. The financial depression hit the US economy hard. It lasted more than five years.

Both Rockefeller and Carnegie made it through the problems caused by the financial depression. But they could not build their empires alone. Their success depended on the laborers in the refineries and steel plants. These workers were growing in number. They were also growing in influence.

CHAPTER TWO

WORK, WORK, WORK

Industrialists like Rockefeller and Carnegie needed laborers. For example, laborers in steel mills operated heavy machinery and tended to the furnaces. Many laborers worked in the same types of jobs for many years. Most laborers were paid low wages and did not have much wealth. They were part of the working class.

Mining, especially for iron and coal, became an important US industry in the mid-1800s.

The Avondale Mine Disaster

In 1869 the Avondale Mine Disaster took place in Pennsylvania. A fire in the mines caused equipment to collapse. The only exit from the tunnel was blocked. All 110 people trapped in the mine died. The next year, Pennsylvania passed a law to protect coal workers. The law said there must be more than one airway for mines.

Miners were also part of the working class. In the mid-1800s, the US mining industry grew quickly. Many new products used coal or iron found underground. But mining was very dangerous. Some underground tunnels caved in and trapped workers. Fires or floods could easily occur in the mines. To make matters worse, miners often faced wage cuts.

Forming a Union

Companies needed to increase profits. Many tried paying laborers lower wages. The workers learned they had a stronger voice if they joined together. They started to form groups called unions. Unions

Striking laborers refused to work until their demands were met. But many employers refused to give in.

worked on behalf of the skilled laborers. In a union, workers could tell their employers they wanted better conditions or more pay. Employers were more likely to take union concerns seriously than issues raised by individual workers.

Sometimes business owners negotiated with unions. If employers would not meet a union's demands, the union could choose to strike. When on strike, all members of the union refused to work until employers gave them what they wanted. With so many workers on strike, little to no work was done at the mines or factories. The businesses did not make money during this time.

Going on Strike

Not all strikes were successful. In early 1875, the Workingmen's Benevolent Association, a coal mining union in Pennsylvania, went on strike. The workers' wages had been cut by about 20 percent. When they stopped working, less coal was mined. But the owners of the company where the miners worked knew the strike was coming. They saved up coal for months.

The owners could sell coal even without their workers. But the strikers could not live without being paid. They stayed on strike for six months. Then they went back to work for less money.

The Centennial Exposition in Philadelphia, Pennsylvania, showed off the newest US technology, including a new type of loom for weaving.

A Time of Invention

Labor wars raged on. But the nation came together in 1876 to mark an important date. It had been 100 years since the signing of the Declaration of Independence. To celebrate, Philadelphia, Pennsylvania, hosted the Centennial Exposition. Since 1851 countries around the world had held world fairs. Each fair showcased the host country for the rest of the world. The Centennial Exposition was the first world's fair hosted by the United States. Technology and innovation were on display. There were more than 30,000 exhibits. At the fair, it was clear the United

An American Inventor

Thomas Alva Edison patented more than 1,000 inventions in his lifetime. As a boy, he was a hard worker. He loved to read and experiment. Edison began inventing in the late 1860s. He set up a laboratory in New Jersey in 1876. There he invented the phonograph and lightbulb. In 1887 Edison built a larger laboratory. Approximately 5,000 people worked there. Edison found ways to record voices. He also made an early moving picture machine. His inventions changed the lives of people all over the world.

States was rising as a world power.

One of the displays was an exciting new tool—the telephone. It allowed people to talk to one another through a wire. They did not have to be close enough to hear each other speak. Alexander Graham Bell and his partner, Thomas A. Watson, developed the telephone earlier in 1876. It was a huge hit. The Bell Telephone Company formed in 1877.

Edison the Inventor

Soon after the telephone was developed, inventor Thomas Edison improved its sound quality. But Edison

Thomas Edison was one of the greatest inventors of the late 1800s.

was also working on another way to communicate. In 1877 he developed the phonograph. This device allowed a person to record a message and then listen to it. Over time the phonograph became a way to listen to music. Edison's invention made him very well known. He set to work on his next project—the lightbulb.

Inventors around the world had been trying to perfect a lightbulb since the 1820s. But all of the attempts cost too much and did not work well enough to be sold on the market. Edison had support from

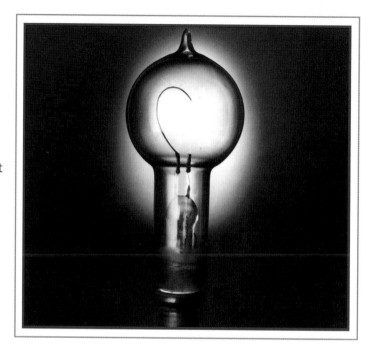

Edison's invention of the incandescent lightbulb changed the world.

J. P. Morgan, a powerful financier. By 1879 Edison had a bulb that could burn for a few hours. The next year, he set up the Edison Electric Illuminating Company of New York.

Lightbulbs could be used in homes, factories, businesses, and to light streets. But Edison knew he also needed power for his lightbulbs. He helped develop a central electric power station. It opened in New York City in 1882. Edison's customers could use his electric lightbulbs instead of gas lamps. And now they had the power to keep the lightbulbs running.

In 1892 workers at Carnegie Steel's Homestead plant went on strike. Carnegie had left his partner in charge of the company. A journalist interviewed Carnegie for the *Pittsburgh Dispatch*:

> THE DISPATCH correspondent asked if [Carnegie] cared to say anything in regard to the troubles at his mills, and Mr. Carnegie, in the most abrupt manner, replied: "I have nothing whatever to say. I have given up all active control of the business, and I don't care to interfere in any way with the present management's conduct of this affair."
>
> . . . "But you must have some opinion in the matter that you are willing to express?"
>
> "No, sir. I am not willing to express any opinion. The men have chosen their course and I am powerless to change it."

Source: "Carnegie Is Seen." Pittsburgh Dispatch *10 July 1892: 1.* Chronicling America: Historic American Newspapers. *Library of Congress. Web. Accessed August 7, 2013.*

Consider Your Audience

The newspaper article was published in Pittsburgh, Pennsylvania, where the strike took place. Knowing this, how do you think the journalist expected his audience to react? Imagine you were one of the workers who went on strike. Write a short poem expressing how you would feel after reading this interview.

CHAPTER THREE

NEW PEOPLE, NEW IDEAS

By the 1880s, Carnegie was at the top of the steel industry. Rockefeller was making a fortune selling oil overseas. These booming industries were boosting the US economy. And people in other countries noticed. The hope of finding work brought many people to the United States.

Before the 1880s, most immigrants to the United States came from northern and western Europe. They

Immigrants from all over the world flooded into the United States in the late 1800s.

were from some of the same places as the first US colonists. In the 1880s and after, more people began coming from southern and eastern Europe, Asia, and other places. They flocked to growing US cities. They brought new languages, traditions, and religions to the country.

The American Way

White immigrants to the United States had a unique problem. They could try to fit in with existing Americans or they could keep a special ethnic identity. Immigrant groups were often stereotyped based on their homeland. These stereotypes could be good or bad. To avoid bad stereotypes, some immigrants chose to break from their group and assimilate, or blend in. Other immigrant groups gained power by staying together.

Discrimination

Americans had mixed feelings about immigration. Many Americans were glad to welcome new people to their country. Others did not like the cultural changes these people brought with them. In some cases, there was now competition for jobs. Chinese immigrants faced discrimination.

Many Chinese immigrants were involved in building US railroads.

Many Chinese came to California in the mid-1800s when gold was discovered there. Others helped build railroads. Many Chinese workers were willing to work for less money. White workers often blamed the Chinese when wages were reduced for all workers.

Many white Americans held racist views about the Chinese immigrants. In 1882 Congress passed the Chinese Exclusion Act. Chinese laborers could no longer enter the United States. The Chinese Exclusion act was not repealed, or canceled, until 1943.

The Chinese were not the only group to face discrimination. Union workers also saw European immigrants as a threat to their jobs. Like the Chinese, many European immigrants were willing to work for low pay. When workers went on strike, some business owners brought in immigrants to work for lower pay.

In the South, slaves were now free. But African Americans still faced racism and discrimination. Few freed slaves owned land where they could run their own farms. As a result, many African Americans still worked on plantations. Whites paid newly freed slaves very little for their labor. African Americans had little power to find better work.

A New Beginning

In 1892 the US government opened a center at Ellis Island, in New York City's harbor. Many immigrants stopped at the island on their way into the United States. There, doctors checked the new immigrants to make sure they were healthy. Each person was asked a few questions. Then the approved immigrants were taken by ferry to New Jersey or New York. Immigrants who failed the checkup were not allowed to enter the United States.

Thousands of people came through Ellis Island each day. From 1892 to 1932, 12 million immigrants passed

A New Kind of Slavery

After the Civil War ended, slavery was outlawed. But Southern landowners still needed workers for their farms. They allowed people to work as sharecroppers on their land. Sharecroppers raised a crop and gave part of it back to the landowner. Sharecroppers were often left with barely enough to survive. They could not save money to buy their own land. Many freed African-American slaves became sharecroppers.

The Statue of Liberty on Bedloe's Island, renamed Liberty Island in 1956, in New York Harbor welcomes new immigrants to the United States.

through Ellis Island. They began new lives in the United States. Some stayed on the East Coast. Others were lured to the West in hope of claiming land.

In 1883 Emma Lazarus wrote the poem "The New Colossus." It eventually appeared on the base of the Statue of Liberty:

> . . .
>
> *A mighty woman with a torch, whose flame*
>
> *Is the imprisoned lightning, and her name*
>
> *Mother of Exiles. From her beacon-hand*
>
> *Glows world-wide welcome; her mild eyes command*
>
> *The air-bridged harbor that twin cities frame.*
>
> *"Keep, ancient lands, your storied pomp!" cries she*
>
> *With silent lips. "Give me your tired, your poor,*
>
> *Your huddled masses yearning to breathe free,*
>
> *The wretched refuse of your teeming shore.*
>
> *Send these, the homeless, tempest-tost to me,*
>
> *I lift my lamp beside the golden door!"*
>
> Source: Emma Lazarus. "The New Colossus." The Poems of Emma Lazarus. *n.p. n.d.* Project Gutenberg. *Web. Accessed August 7, 2013.*

What's the Big Idea?

Read this poem carefully. Based on the poem, how do you think Lazarus felt about immigration?

CHAPTER FOUR

A WORLD POWER

Congress passed the Homestead Act in 1862. It provided land to people hoping to move west. In the 1870s and 1880s, settlers poured into the Great Plains region. They wanted to establish homesteads. Many of these settlers were immigrants. They were excited about the prospect of owning land and farms. But life on the Great Plains was not

In the late 1800s, many settlers began moving to the Great Plains of the western United States.

The invention of barbed wire changed the cattle industry in the West.

easy. Wood for building was hard to find. Periods of drought made watering crops difficult.

Many settlers who moved west hoped to start farms and ranches. Their animals could graze on the grasses of the wide-open Great Plains. But they had

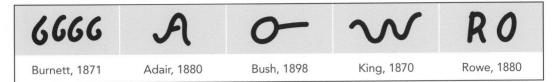

6666	A	O—	w	RO
Burnett, 1871	Adair, 1880	Bush, 1898	King, 1870	Rowe, 1880

Cattle Brands

Ranchers use branding to mark an animal with a symbol. The symbol lets others know who owns the animal. Cattle were often branded with a hot iron. Study this chart of five well-known brands, or symbols, from the 1800s. What do you think the shapes represent? How might these shapes relate to the cattle industry? Branding is not often used today. Find out how modern ranchers identify their cattle.

no way to keep their animals on their land. This was because on the prairies there were few trees to make wood fences. In 1874 barbed wire was patented. Cattle owners now had what they needed to fence the open prairies. The government owned most of the land. Cattle owners started putting up fences on public land. They wanted to keep their animals in and other people and animals out. The fences angered people who wanted to start their own farms and homesteads. The cattle ate much of the grass. It was slow to grow back. This led to a shortage of food for other animals.

Still, by the late 1800s, cattle ranching was a major industry. The developing railroads took meat from the ranches to the cities on the east coast.

Western Settlement and Native Americans

Another issue facing settlers was frequent clashes with Native Americans. In the 1820s, the US government began forcing many eastern Native-American tribes to move. They were sent to a region known as Indian Territory. This area made up most of present-day Oklahoma. By 1880 it was home to the Cherokee, Creek, Seminole, Chickasaw, and many other tribes. As more settlers came to the West, they wanted to move onto this Native-American land. Some settlers entered the land illegally to live on it.

Many settlers believed Native Americans would be better off if they assimilated into mainstream culture. In 1887 Congress passed the Dawes Act. The act broke up Native American tribes by giving land to individual families for farming. But Native

In 1889 thousands of settlers swarmed the plains of Oklahoma to build homesteads on Native-American land.

Americans had always lived as tribal communities. Many had been hunters and did not know how to farm. Congress issued the Indian Appropriations Act in 1889. This act opened Indian Territory to settlers. Men and women rushed into the area to claim land that had once belonged to the Native Americans.

A Change in Farming

By the late 1800s, farming was still an important industry in the United States. But new technologies were changing US farming. Better transportation

The Populist Movement

To help solve their problems, farmers in the Midwest and South banded together in groups called Farmers' Alliances. In 1892 the Farmers' Alliances reorganized into the Populist Party. It supported more government assistance for farmers. The party wanted to put farmers on more equal footing with businesses and industries. The Populist Party did not achieve all its goals. But several of its members were elected to Congress. The party also convinced lawmakers to pass some laws that would help farmers. In 1896 the party became less common. The Democratic Party took up many of the Populist Party's ideas.

meant goods could be shipped between states and countries. The goods were sometimes cheaper in one place than in another. Not all farmers could compete with these lower prices. Railroads charged farmers high prices to ship their goods. Many farmers took loans from banks. They went into debt paying for seeds, farm equipment, and transportation. If a farmer could not pay the loan, the bank often took the farm.

Some farmers left their land for jobs in cities.

Others chose to change the way they farmed. For example, Northeast farmers began to focus on dairy farming. Milk, butter, and cheese were needed in the big cities on the east coast. Better refrigeration allowed the farmers to keep their products cold longer.

War with Spain

As farmers struggled to find their place in the US economy, tensions were taking place outside the nation as well. The United States was facing conflict with Spain. Spain controlled the Caribbean island of Cuba. But the Cubans wanted independence. The United States sided with

Farming Technologies

Barbed wire and improved refrigeration were just two of the new devices that made farming easier in the late 1800s. Mechanical planters helped farmers plant seeds more quickly than hand tools. Farmers used reapers and binders to harvest grain. These devices cut the grain and tied it together. Similar devices became common for harvesting corn crops. In 1892 the first gasoline tractor was built. But gas-powered tractors would not take off until the 1900s.

A lifeboat rescues survivors from the USS *Maine* after its explosion in 1898. The United States blamed Spain for the explosion, triggering the Spanish-American War.

Cuba. When a US ship blew up in a Cuban harbor in February 1898, US newspapers blamed Spain.

The two nations declared war on one another in April. In May the US Navy defeated the Spanish fleet in the Philippines. In July US troops landed in Cuba and defeated the Spanish there. A peace treaty was signed in December. The United States kept temporary control of Cuba while it set up a government. The island gained full independence in 1902. The United States also gained control of the

FURTHER EVIDENCE

Chapter Four covers many topics, including moving Native Americans to new land. What was one of the chapter's main points about this topic? How does the author support this point? Visit the Web site at the link below. Find a quote about how the US government moved Native Americans to new land. Write a few sentences about how the information on the Web site relates to the author's point in this chapter.

Andrew Jackson and the Indian Removal Treaties

www.mycorelibrary.com/rise-of-industry

Philippines, Puerto Rico, and Guam. These places had also been controlled by Spain.

Spain was a powerful European country. The United States' victory in the Spanish-American War proved the nation had become a world power. After decades of railroad growth and booming industry, the United States was set to enter the twentieth century on strong footing.

IMPORTANT DATES

1869

On May 10, two railroads join in Promontory, Utah, forming the US transcontinental railroad.

1870

John D. Rockefeller founds the Standard Oil Company.

1873

A major bank failure causes a financial panic and economic depression.

1879

Thomas Edison develops a lightbulb that can burn for a few hours.

1882

US Congress passes the Chinese Exclusion Act.

1887

Congress passes the Dawes Act, breaking up Native-American tribes and urging them to become farmers.

1875

A strike by the Workingmen's Benevolent Association, a coal mining union, fails.

1876

Alexander Graham Bell and Thomas A. Watson develop the telephone.

1876

Philadelphia, Pennsylvania, hosts the Centennial Exposition.

1889

The Indian Appropriations Act opens Indian Territory to settlers.

1892

Ellis Island opens.

1898

The US defeats Spain in the Spanish-American War.

STOP AND THINK

You Are There

Imagine you are a child immigrating to the United States through Ellis Island in the late 1800s. You hear Emma Lazarus's poem being read aloud as you view the Statue of Liberty. How does the poem make you feel? What words or phrases cause those feelings? Answer these questions in a short journal entry.

Take a Stand

People who lived in the United States in the late 1800s had many views about immigrants. Some welcomed them, but others saw them as a threat to jobs and US ways of life. What do you think about immigration today? Should the United States encourage immigration or limit it? Write a short essay explaining your opinion.

Say What?

Reading a book often means there are new words to learn. There are many business terms in this book. Find five words about business in this book that are new to you. Look up their meanings in a dictionary. Then try to use each word in a sentence.

Another View

Labor unions earned many victories for workers in the 1800s. Ask an adult, such as a librarian, to help you research the labor unions of today. What do today's unions represent? How are unions helpful? Do unions have any negative effects on workers and employers?

GLOSSARY

assimilate
to blend in and become like other people

discrimination
the act of treating people differently because of their ethnicity, gender, or religion

financier
a person who deals with large amounts of money

fleet
a group of ships belonging to a country

homesteads
plots of land granted by the US government where people could build their own homes

innovation
a new idea

mainstream
popular, common

negotiate
to discuss an issue with the hope of resolving it in a way that makes multiple people or groups happy

refinery
a place where a product is processed

stereotypes
characteristics associated with a group

strike
a work stoppage, often organized by a union

union
a group of workers who join together for a common cause

LEARN MORE

Books

Gomez, Rebecca. *Thomas Edison*. Edina, MN: ABDO, 2003.

Hernández, Roger E. *The Spanish-American War*. New York: Marshall Cavendish, 2010.

Murdoch, David Hamilton. *North American Indian*. New York: DK in association with the American Museum of Natural History, 2005.

Web Links

To learn more about the rise of industry in the United States, visit ABDO Publishing Company online at **www.abdopublishing.com**. Web sites about the rise of industry are featured on our Book Links page. These links are routinely monitored and updated to provide the most current information available.

Visit **www.mycorelibrary.com** for free additional tools for teachers and students.

INDEX

ABOUT THE AUTHOR

Amy Van Zee is an editor and writer who lives with her family near Minneapolis, Minnesota. She has an English degree from the University of Minnesota and has contributed to dozens of educational books.